Internet Use and Openness to Trade

David Riker [1]

U.S. International Trade Commission, Office of Economics

December 15, 2014

Abstract

This paper presents an econometric model that links the number of broadband users in a country to its volume of international trade in goods and services. The model indicates that the growth in broadband use between 2000 and 2011 increased a country's openness to trade (measured by the ratio of their total trade to their GDP) by 4.21 percentage points on average, with much larger effects in high income countries (a 10.21 percentage point increase on average) than in developing countries (a 1.67 percentage point increase on average). We also use the econometric model to project how each country's openness to trade will be affected by expected future growth in broadband use: we project that the trade-to-GDP ratios will increase an additional 6.88 percentage points on average in the high income countries and an additional 1.67 percentage points on average in the developing countries due to further growth in broadband use over the next five years.

Keywords: International Trade, Openness, Internet, Broadband, Econometrics

JEL Classification: F14, F15, O31

---

[1] This working paper is the result of ongoing professional research of ITC Staff and is solely meant to represent the opinions and professional research of the author. It is not meant to represent in any way the views of the U.S. International Trade Commission or any of its individual Commissioners. I would like to thank D. Coffin, M. Lawless, and A. Butcher for helpful comments and suggestions. Please address any correspondence to David.Riker@usitc.gov.

1. Introduction

Openness to trade increased between 2000 and 2012. Figure 1 reports the median value of the ratio of each country's total trade in goods and services to the country's GDP for each year. This ratio is a common measure of a country's integration into the global economy.[2] As Figure 1 shows, the upward trend in openness was interrupted by the global economic downturn in 2009 and 2010, but the upward trend has reemerged.

In this paper, we examine whether this increase in openness can be attributed, at least in part, to reductions in trade costs. As Anderson and van Wincoop (2004) explain, there are many types of costs that impede international trade, including transportation costs, policy barriers, information costs, legal and regulatory costs, currency costs, and local distribution costs. While freight costs, tariffs and logistical bottlenecks are significant barriers to trade in many countries, they have not changed significantly over the last decade. In contrast, information costs have fallen dramatically, and this has probably contributed to the rise in countries' openness to trade.

Figure 2 reports the 25th, 50th, and 75th percentile values for the number of broadband users per 100 people in 148 countries for each year between 2000 and 2012. The 148 countries have adopted the new technology at very different rates. While the 75th percentile rose from zero to 15 per 100 people over the thirteen years, the 25th percentile value remained below 1 per 100 people at the end of the period. Broadband use is much more common in high income countries than in developing countries. In 2012, the average number of broadband users per 100 people was 23.55 in high income countries, 8.20 in upper middle income countries, 2.17 in lower middle income countries, and 2.10 in low income countries.

We utilize this variation in broadband growth across the countries to quantify the contribution of the growth in broadband use to the expansion in international trade. We estimate a set of multivariate regression models that control for economic factors that have affected the countries' openness to trade. We find that there is a positive relationship between broadband use and a country's openness to trade that is statistically and economically significant.

Section 2 reviews the growing literature on the link between a country's Internet use and its openness to trade. Our study adopts features of the models in the literature, but it also contributes

---

[2] For example, this measure is used in di Giovanni and Levchenko (2009), di Giovanni, Levchenko and Rancière (2011), Ramondo and Rodríguez-Clare (2013), and many other economic studies.

several innovations. Section 3 describes our econometric methodology, and Section 4 reports parameter estimates for alternative econometric specifications.

Then we apply the econometric model in backward-looking and forward-looking analyses of the link between broadband use and openness to trade. Section 5 calculates the historical contribution of the growth in broadband use between 2000 and 2011 to the increase in the countries' openness to trade over these years. Section 6 projects the future increases in openness that we expect from further expansion of broadband use over the next five years. Section 7 offers concluding remarks.

2. Literature on the Economic Link between the Internet and International Trade

The economic literature on the contribution of the Internet to international trade has grown significantly over the last decade. Two early studies by Freund and Weinhold are seminal contributions to this literature. Freund and Weinhold (2002) estimate the effect of Internet penetration on the growth in a country's trade in services, controlling for GDP growth and exchange rate fluctuations. Their econometric model utilizes data from the U.S. Bureau of Economic Analysis on U.S. cross-border exports of services between 1995 and 1999. Their measure of a country's Internet penetration is the number of Internet host sites identified with the country. They estimate that a 10 percentage point increase in Internet penetration would result in a 1.7 percentage point increase in the growth of a country's exports of services and a 1.1 percentage point increase in the growth in the country's imports of services. They find that these trade effects are largest for business, professional, and technical services. In a companion article, Freund and Weinhold (2004), they find that the Internet also increased trade in goods. They estimate an econometric model with annual export growth as the dependent variable. Their model indicates that the Internet contributed one percentage point to annual export growth on average in their panel of 56 countries between 1997 and 1999.[3]

This early work by Freund and Weinhold were followed by several econometric studies that refined the methodology and updated the data to reflect the continued rapid growth in Internet use. Clarke and Wallsten (2006) utilize cross-sectional data on the total exports of goods in 2001 for 26 high income countries and 72 developing countries. Their econometric model distinguishes between high income countries and developing countries. They use instrumental variables to address

---

[3] They also report an econometric model in which the log of each country's trade-to-GDP ratio is the dependent variable. The second model also indicates that there were significant positive effects of Internet penetration on trade in goods in 1998 and 1999.

potential endeneity bias.[4] They find that there were significant positive effects of the Internet on the export flows from developing countries to high income countries, but only when they instrument for Internet use.[5] Vemuri and Siddiqi (2009) is an econometric analysis of a panel of 64 countries between 1985 and 2005. They find that communications infrastructure and Internet use had a positive and significant effect on international trade. Choi (2010) estimates the effects of Internet use on countries' exports of services using a panel of 151 countries between 1990 and 2006. His model indicates that a doubling of Internet usage would increase a country's exports of services by 2 to 4 percent. Liu and Nath (2013) focus on the use of the Internet in 40 emerging market economies between 1995 and 2010. They find that Internet subscriptions and Internet hosts had significant positive effects on the countries' exports and imports of goods.

Lendle, Olarreaga, Schropp, and Vézina (2012) takes a very different approach to estimating the contribution of the Internet to international trade: they use transaction-level data to estimate a set of gravity models that distinguish between international trade flows that were executed on the eBay on-line platform and transactions through conventional, off-line channels. Using data on U.S. exports to 62 countries between 2004 and 2007, they estimate that the negative effect of international distance on trade is 65 percent smaller (in absolute value) on the eBay on-line platform. This is an interesting study, but it is difficult to extrapolate from their findings to the broader effects of the Internet on aggregate international trade flows, since the cross-border transactions on eBay represent less than 0.1 percent of total international trade.

U.S. International Trade Commission (2014) finds that the Internet has significantly reduced international trade costs. The study presents an econometric model that estimates that Internet use reduces trade costs for U.S. imports and exports of digitally intensive goods and services by 26 percent on average. The study also reports the outcome of a survey of thousands of U.S. firms in digitally intensive industries.[6]

Table 1 compares the basic features and findings of these eight studies. To summarize, the econometric studies vary greatly in the time periods that they cover, the way that they measure

---

[4] The main instrument for their measure of Internet use is an indicator for whether the country had a legal monopoly in data transmission services.

[5] Clarke and Wallsten also estimate a gravity model of the countries' bilateral exports. The gravity model indicates that there was also an effect on trade between developing countries.

[6] The survey respondents indicated that the Internet increases international trade by facilitating internal and business-to-business communications, advertising, and marketing. The survey respondents also indicated that the Internet has a significant positive effect on the productivity of U.S. firms in digitally intensive industries.

Internet use, the types of trade flows that they are modeling, and the technical details of their methodologies, but they all find that the growth of the Internet has had a significant positive effect on international trade.

3. Methodology

We estimated an econometric model that adopts features of the models in this literature but also contributes several innovations. Equation (1) represents the economic relationship between a country's openness and its number of broadband users.

$$TO_{j,t} = \alpha_j + \beta_t + \gamma\, U_{j,t-1} + \varepsilon_{j,t} \tag{1}$$

The variable $TO_{j,t}$ is the openness of country j in year t, defined as the ratio of the country's total trade in goods and services to its GDP. The variable α_j represents a set of country fixed effects. They control for institutional factors that affect trade (including infrastructure and trade policies) and natural barriers to trade (including distance, remoteness, and language) that vary substantially across countries but were for the most part fixed in each country between 2000 and 2012.[7] The variable β_t represents a set of year fixed effects. They control for global factors that vary over time but were for the most part common across countries, like the economic downturn in 2009. The variable $U_{j,t-1}$ is the number of broadband users per 100 people in country j in year $t - 1$. We use the lagged value of the broadband measure in the model to mitigate concerns about potential endogeneity bias.[8] The variable $\varepsilon_{j,t}$ is a normally distributed error term.

Equation (2) is an alternative version of the model that allows the coefficient on $U_{j,t-1}$ to vary by country and year: in this case, the broadband term is the product of the number of broadband users in country j and a GDP-weighted average of the number of broadband users in all countries other than j, multiplied by the parameter γ.

$$TO_{j,t} = \alpha_j + \beta_t + \gamma\left(\sum_{k \neq j} \omega_{k,t-1}\, U_{k,t-1}\right) U_{j,t-1} + \varepsilon_{j,t} \tag{2}$$

---

[7] The studies that are summarized in Table 1 use several different methods for controlling for country fixed effects. For example, the dependent variable in the model in Freund and Weinhold (2004) is the export growth rate, and this effectively differences out country fixed effects. Clarke and Wallsten (2006), on the other hand, include many country-level covariates to try to control for differences in exporting across the countries that are not due to differences in Internet use. Liu and Nath (2013) include country dummy variables in their econometric models.

[8] Several of the studies in the literature, including Vemuri and Siddiqi (2009) and Choi (2010), use lagged values of their Internet measure to address this concern. We also report estimates based on contemporaneous values as a sensitivity analysis.

We expect that high rates of broadband use in one country have a greater effect on its openness if its trade partners also have high rates of broadband use, reflecting network effects.[9] The variable k in equation (2) is an index of countries, and $\omega_{k,t-1}$ is country k's share of the combined GDPs of all countries other than j in year $t-1$.

The measures of broadband users and openness are from the World Bank's World Development Indicators database. The econometric models are estimated from a panel of 148 countries over a 12-year period from 2001 to 2012.[10] Table 2 reports descriptive statistics for the data that we use. There is a fair amount of variation in the trade-to-GDP ratios. The overall coefficient of variation is equal to 0.59.[11] Most of the variation in this measure of openness is cross-sectional: within-year variation across countries accounts for almost all of the variation in the trade-to-GDP ratio. There is even more variation in the measure of broadband use. The coefficient of variation for this measure is equal to 1.75. Most of the variation in this measure occurs within each country over time.

The alternative econometric specifications in equations (1) and (2) impose the pooling restriction that the same regression coefficient applies to all 148 countries in all of the years. However, the country and year effects in the model accommodate much of the heterogeneity in the data, and the variable coefficient on $U_{j,t-1}$ in equation (2) provides additional flexibility across countries and over time.[12]

4. Econometric Estimates

Table 3 reports the OLS estimates of the model parameters for four different econometric specifications based on equations (1) and (2). The four models all have the same dependent variable, the country's total trade as a share of its GDP, and they all explain approximately 94 percent of the variation in this measure according to the R^2 statistics. There is a significant positive effect of broadband use an openness in all four models. The Akaike Information Criterion (AIC) at the bottom of the table compares the fit of the models, while adjusting for the number of

---

[9] U.S. International Trade Commission (2014) considers this type of interaction between Internet user rates. The other studies in Table 1 only include the country's own use of the Internet as an explanatory variable.

[10] The estimation sample includes the 148 countries with complete or almost complete data on the number of Internet users. Where there were missing values for the years prior to very low initial values, these missing values were coded as zeroes.

[11] The coefficient of variation is defined as the ratio of the standard deviation of the measure to its mean.

[12] We also consider less restrictive alternatives in our sensitivity analysis.

parameters that are estimated.[13] Model 4, which includes the variable coefficient on $U_{j,t-1}$ and year fixed effects, is the preferred specification because it has the lowest AIC value and the largest R^2 statistic.[14] In Model 4, the point estimate of γ is 0.0194, with a robust standard error of 0.0039. This estimate implies that an increase in the number of broadband users *in all countries* by 10 per 100 people would increase the countries' trade-to-GDP ratios by 1.94 percentage points on average. Wald tests indicate that the country fixed effects and year fixed effects in the models are statistically significant.

Table 4 reports a series of sensitivity tests of the preferred specification in Model 4. The tests address potential concerns about omitted variables, endogeneity, and pooling restrictions. The first test adds the relative size of the country (measured as its share of world GDP) as an explanatory variable for openness. This addresses potential omitted variable bias in Model 4. The additional variable is not individually significant, its inclusion raises the AIC, and its inclusion does not have a notable effect on the estimate of γ. For all of these reasons, this addition does not improve the econometric model.

The second sensitivity test adds an indicator for whether the country was a member of the WTO in the particular year. In general, we expect that the country fixed effects in the models will control for differences in trade policy regimes across countries, since these policies were steady over the estimation period. However, some of the countries joined the WTO during the period, and this significant change likely had a positive effect on their openness to trade. However, adding this explanatory variable has almost no effect on the estimated coefficient on the broadband measure: it increases the estimate of γ from 0.0194 to 0.0196. The additional variable is not statistically significant and including it raises the AIC relative to Model 4, so this addition also does not improve the econometric model.

The third sensitivity test relaxes the pooling restrictions in Model 4. It allows for different values of γ for high income countries and for developing countries. This variation on Model 4 addresses the indications from Clarke and Wallsten (2006) and Liu and Nath (2013) that there are larger effects of the Internet on the trade of developing countries than on the trade of high income countries. When the pooling restriction is relaxed, the point estimate of γ is larger for the high income

---

[13] The AIC is equal to $2p - 2ln(LF)$. The variable p is the number of parameters of the model, and the variable LF is the likelihood function.

[14] This is the specification in equation (2), in which high rates of broadband use in one country have a greater effect on its volume of trade if its trade partners also have high rates of broadband use.

countries (0.0195) than for the developing countries (0.0159), the opposite of the ranking in the earlier studies. However, a Wald test cannot reject the null hypothesis that the two coefficients are equal, so this negative test result supports the pooling restriction that is imposed in Model 4.

The final sensitivity test replaces the lagged values of the broadband measure with contemporaneous values. The estimate based on the contemporaneous values is smaller but similar (the estimated coefficient is 0.0176, compared to 0.0194 in Model 4), and the fit of the alternative model is worse (the AIC is higher).

5. Historical Contribution to the Increase in Openness

Next, we use the econometric model to calculate the historical contributions of the increases in broadband users to the changes in the countries' openness between 2001 and 2012. The historical contribution to the openness of country j, HC_j, is defined as:

$$HC_j = 0.0194 \left[U_{j,2011} \left(\sum_{k \neq j} \omega_{k,2011} U_{k,2011} \right) - U_{j,2000} \left(\sum_{k \neq j} \omega_{k,2000} U_{k,2000} \right) \right] \qquad (3)$$

Table 5 reports the increases in the countries' trade-to-GDP ratios due to the historical increases in broadband users between 2001 and 2012. The average increase across the 148 countries is 4.21 percentage points. The historical contribution to openness is positive or zero for all of the countries over the period, since the change in the number of broadband users is positive or zero. Nevertheless, there is significant variation in the size of HC_j across the 148 countries. The effect of the historical increases in broadband users ranges from no effect in many of the developing countries to an increase of 17.34 percentage points in Switzerland. The average increase is 10.21 percentage points for the high income countries but only 1.67 percentage points for the developing countries. The magnitude for each country depends on the increase in its number of broadband users over the period. Table 5 reports the ten countries with the largest historical contributions. Switzerland, the Netherlands, Denmark, and Korea are at the top of the list.

The last column in Table 5 reports the total net increases in the trade-to-GDP ratios between 2001 and 2012. In most countries, the increase in broadband users added to the rise in their openness to trade. In a few countries, those with a net decline in their trade-to-GDP ratio, the increase in broadband users partly offset their decline.

As a sensitivity analysis, we recalculated the historical contributions using alternate Model 2 from Table 3. This alternative model does not include the variable coefficient on $U_{j,t-1}$. Table 6 compares the two sets of estimates. The average increases based on Model 2 are 13 to 15 percent lower than the average increases based on Model 4.

6. Potential Effects If the Developing Countries Were to Catch Up

The same model and data are also indicative of the potential for further increases in openness to trade as broadband use continues to expand in the future. The number of broadband users in the 104 developing countries in the dataset ranged from 0 to 22.20 users per 100 people in 2012, with an average of 3.72 per 100 people. This was substantially lower than the number of broadband users in Switzerland, the leader in 2012 at 40.10 per 100 people. This gap suggests that there are large potential increases in the openness of the developing countries, for example if they were to catch up to Switzerland's level of broadband use.

We can use the model to quantify the potential increase in openness in the developing countries in the model *assuming this hypothetical catchup*.[15] The potential increases are inversely related to the calculations of historical contributions in Table 5. For countries with large historical contributions, there may be less room for future growth, since $U_{j,t-1}$ may be already approaching its practical limit. On the other hand, for developing countries with essentially no broadband users in 2012, there is great potential for increasing openness according to the model. The "catch up" increase is simply the difference between the historical contribution to openness in the leader (Switzerland, 17.05 percentage points) and the historical contribution to openness in the particular country (in some cases, zero).

If all of the countries in the model were to increase their number of broadband users to Switzerland's 40.10 per 100 people, then the point estimate of γ in Model 4 implies that the trade-to-GDP ratios would rise by 29.52 percentage points on average in the 104 developing countries. The increases would range from 21.23 to 31.20 percentage points, depending on the country's number of broadband users in 2012. If we use the estimate of γ that is specific to the developing countries (0.0159, according to the sensitivity test in Table 4), then the trade-to-GDP ratios would rise by 24.20 percentage points on average, with a range from 17.40 to 25.57 percentage points.

---

[15] The econometric model does not tell us *how* or *if* these developing countries could catch up to the leader (e.g., whether this could occur simply by increasing income levels or whether it would require public infrastructure investments or changes in regulation in the country).

7. Projections of the Future Effects on Openness to Trade

Finally, we use the econometric model to project future increases in openness as the countries continue to increase their number of broadband users. This calculation is a *forecast*, in contrast to the assessment of potential (but hypothetical) catchup in Section 6. Projecting the increases in openness requires a forecast of the growth of each country's broadband use in future years. These forecasts are based on the following econometric model:

$$U_{j,t} - U_{j,t} = \delta + \theta\, U_{j,t-1} + \lambda\, RGDPPC_{j,t} + \eta_{j,t} \tag{4}$$

The variable $U_{j,t}$ is again the number of broadband users per 100 people in country j in year t, $RGDPPC_{j,t}$ is the country's real GDP per capita (a conventional indicator of a country's level of economic development), and $\eta_{j,t}$ is a normally distributed error term. It is clear from the data that broadband use has grown faster and achieved much higher coverage in high income countries than in developing countries, so we expect that $\lambda > 0$. Table 7 reports four sets of parameter estimates based on equation (4), with different exclusion restrictions imposed on the parameters of the model. The econometric estimates indicate that Model 7, in which the year-to-year increase in the number of broadband users is related to the country's GDP per capita but is not related to the lagged number of broadband users, is the preferred model. It has the lowest AIC value and the highest R^2 statistic. In Model 7, there are larger average increases in the high income countries: the point estimate of λ is 0.0041 (with a standard error of 0.0003). The estimate of δ is 0.2994 (with a standard error of 0.0274).

We use these parameter estimates and forecasted values of $RGDPPC_{j,t}$ from the IMF's World Economic Outlook (WEO) database to forecast the number of broadband users in country j in future year F as follows:

$$U_{j,F} = U_{j,2012} + 0.2994\,(F - 2012) + \sum_{t=2012}^{F} 0.0041\, RGDPPC_{j,t} \tag{5}$$

Then we use forecasted GDP shares of the countries from the WEO database, along with the forecasted numbers of broadband users, to project the countries' trade-to-GDP ratio ahead five years to 2017. The projected future effect on the openness of country j, PF_j, is equal to:

$$PF_j = 0.0194 \left[U_{j,2016} \left(\sum_{k \neq j} \omega_{k,2016}\, U_{k,2016} \right) - U_{j,2011} \left(\sum_{k \neq j} \omega_{k,2011}\, U_{k,2011} \right) \right] \tag{6}$$

Table 8 reports the projected five-year increases in the number of broadband users per 100 people, as well as the projected future increases in openness in the 142 countries.[16] The average projected increase in the countries' trade-to-GDP ratio is 3.20 percentage points. Again, there is significant variation across the countries. The increases in trade-to-GDP ratio range from no effect (in developing countries that still had almost no broadband users in 2012) to an increase of 13.40 percentage points in Luxembourg. The average increase is 6.88 percentage points for the high income countries but only 1.67 percentage points for the developing countries.

8. Conclusions

There has been a dramatic increase in broadband connectivity over the last decade. Our model suggests that these improvements in communication infrastructure have had a positive impact on international trade that is economically significant (the effects on the trade-to-GDP ratios are fairly large) and statistically significant (the effects on trade-to-GDP ratios are fairly precisely estimated). We are able to statistically estimate these effects, and separate them from confounding factors, because the growth in broadband use has been dramatic and has varied widely across the countries.

These effects are qualitatively similar to the effects reported in the literature reviewed in Section 2, despite differences in the study period, data, and estimation technique. In terms of quantitative estimates, the studies in the literature typically report the magnitudes of these effects as elasticities or impact coefficients.[17] In this paper, we followed their lead by presenting the econometric estimates in terms of an impact coefficient – we estimate that an increase in the number of broadband users in all countries by 10 per 100 people *would* increase the countries' trade-to-GDP ratios by 1.94 percentage points on average –but we go further by using the econometric model to calculate the historical contributions of the increases in broadband use, and then to project future growth.

In both of these applications, large increases in broadband use translate into increases in trade-to-GDP ratios equal to several percentage points. The model suggests that the historical growth in broadband use between 2000 and 2011 *did increase* the countries' openness to trade (measured by

---

[16] A few countries were not included in these forward-looking calculations because the WEO database did not forecast their GDP and GDP per capita.

[17] For example, Freund and Weinhold (2002) estimate that a 10 percent increase in Internet penetration would increase a country's growth in services exports by 1.7 percentage points, and Choi (2012) estimates that a doubling of Internet usage in a country would lead to a 2 to 4 percent increase in services trade.

the ratio of their total trade to their GDP) by 4.21 percentage points on average, with larger effects in the high income countries (a 10.21 percentage point increase on average) than in the developing countries (a 1.67 percentage point increase on average). The increases in broadband users that we project through 2016 suggest that the countries' trade-to-GDP ratios *will increase* by an additional 6.88 percentage points on average in the high income countries and by an additional 1.67 percentage points on average in the developing countries.

References

Anderson, J.E. and E. van Wincoop (2004): "Trade Costs." *Journal of Economic Literature* 42: 691-751.

Choi, C. (2010): "The Effect of the Internet on Services Trade." *Economic Letters* 109: 102-104.

Clarke, G.R.G. and S.J. Wallsten (2006): "Has the Internet Increased Trade? Developed and Developing Country Evidence." *Economic Inquiry* 44 (3): 465-484.

di Giovanni, J. and A.A. Levchenko (2009): "Trade Openness and Volatility." *Review of Economics and Statistics* 91 (3): 558-585.

di Giovanni, J, A.A. Levchenko and R. Rancière (2011): "Power Laws in Firm Size and Openness to Trade: Measurement and Implications." *Journal of International Economics* 85: 42-52.

Freund, C. and D. Weinhold (2002): "The Internet and International Trade in Services." *American Economic Review Papers and Proceedings* 92 (2): 236-240.

Freund, C. and D. Weinhold (2004): "The Effect of the Internet on International Trade." *Journal of International Economics* 62: 171-189.

Lendle, A., M. Olarreaga, S. Schropp and P. Vézina (2012): "There Goes Gravity: How eBay Reduces Trade Costs." World Bank Policy Research Working Paper 6253.

Liu, L. and H.K. Nath (2013): "Information and Communications Technology and Trade in Emerging Market Economies." *Emerging Markets Finance & Trade* 49 (6): 67-87.

Ramondo, N. and A. Rodríguez-Clare (2013): "Trade, Multinational Production, and the Gains from Openness." *Journal of Political Economy* 121(2): 273-322.

U.S. International Trade Commission (2014): *Digital Trade in the U.S. and Global Economies, Part 2.* Publication No. 4485. Washington, DC.

Vemuri, V.K. and S. Siddiqi (2009): "Impact of Commercialization of the Internet on International Trade: A Panel Study Using the Extended Gravity Model." *International Trade Journal* 23 (4): 458-484.

Figure 1. Median of the Openness Ratio (Total Trade as a Share of GDP)

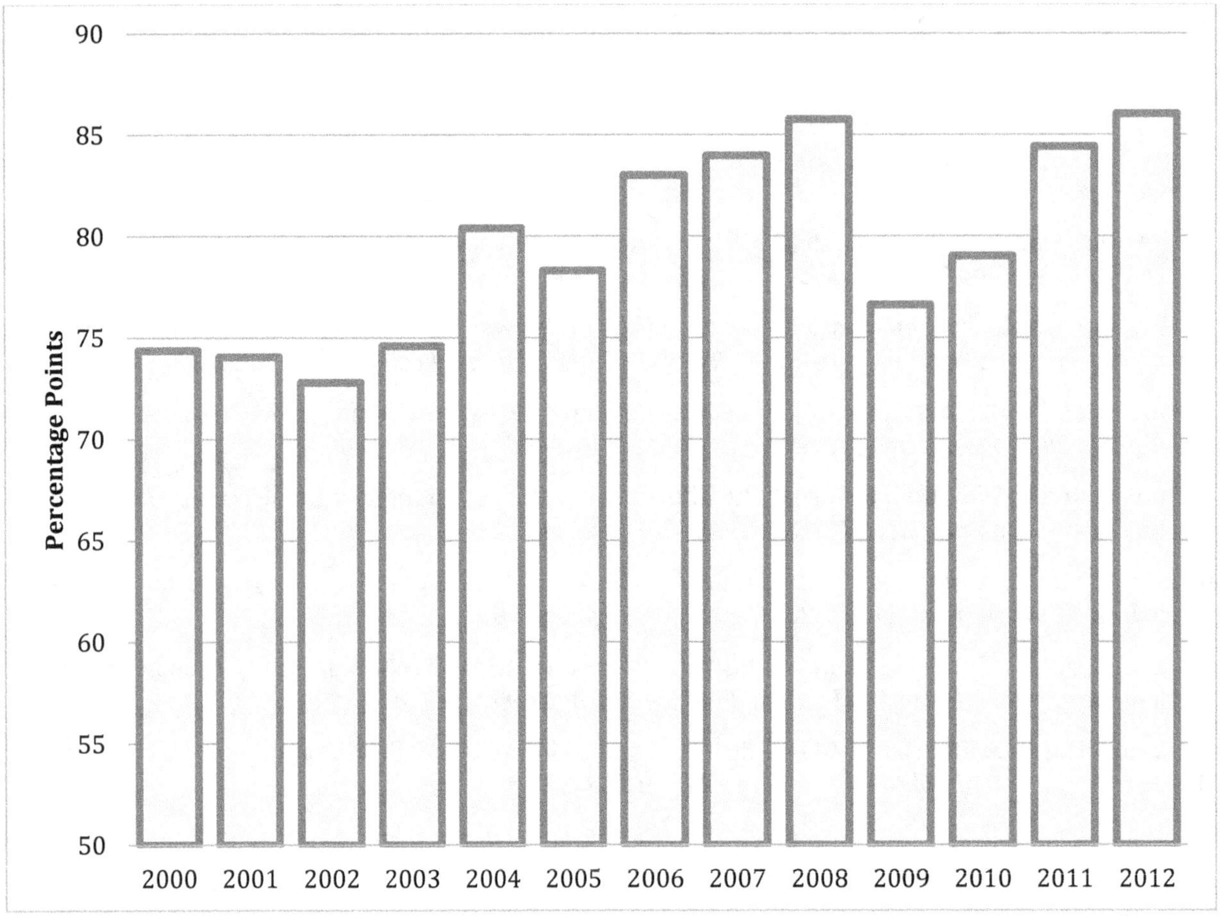

Figure 2. Broadband Use per 100 People

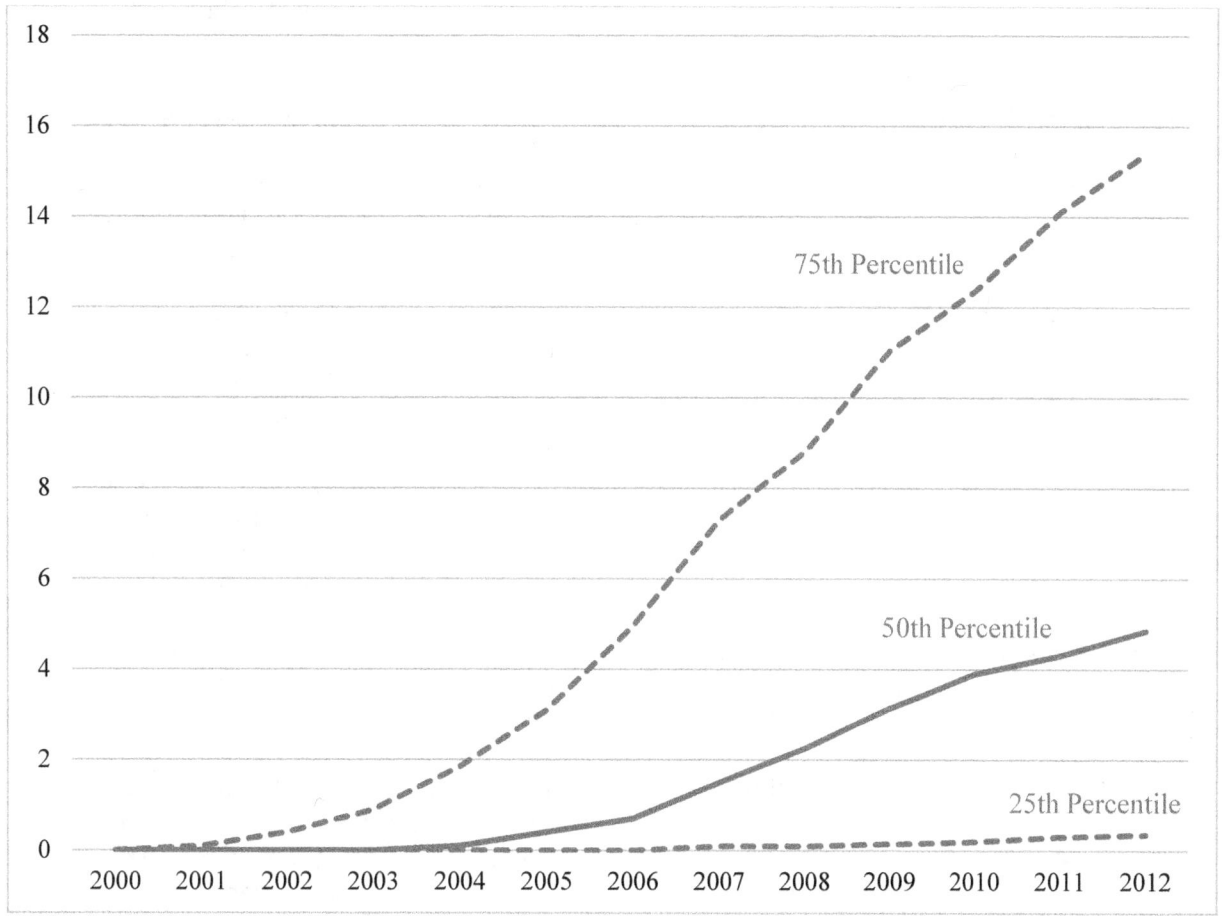

Table 1. Findings in the Literature

Authors	Internet Measure	Study Period	Specific Quantitative Estimates
Freund and Weinhold (2002)	Internet Hosts	1995 to 1999	A 10 percent increase in Internet penetration increases a country's growth in services exports by 1.7 percentage points.
Freund and Weinhold (2004)	Internet Hosts	1997 to 1999	The Internet contributed one percentage point to annual growth in exports of goods from 1997 to 1999.
Clarke and Wallsten (2006)	Internet Hosts	2001	A one percent increase in Internet hosts increases exports to high-come countries by 0.4 percent.
Vemuri and Siddiqi (2009)	Internet Users per 100 People	1985 to 2005	Not reported.
Choi (2010)	Internet Users per 100 People	1990 to 2006	A doubling of Internet usage in a country would lead to a 2 to 4 percent increase in services trade.
Lendle, Olarreaga et al. (2012)	Transacted on eBay	2004 to 2007	The effect of distance on international trade was 65 percent smaller on the on-line platform
Liu and Nath (2013)	Multiple ICT Measures	1995 to 2010	Internet subscriptions and hosts have significant positive effects on exports in emerging markets. They do not report a specific elasticity or impact coefficient.
U.S. International Trade Commission (2014)	Internet Users per 100 People	2011	The Internet reduces the trade costs for U.S. imports and exports of digitally intensives services by 26 percent on average.

Table 2. Descriptive Statistics for the Data (2000-2012)

Explanatory Variables	Mean	St. Dev.	Minimum	Maximum
Openness (Total Trade as a Share of GDP)	89.77	53.16	18.04	449.99
Number of Broadband Users per 100 People	5.05	8.83	0.00	40.10
Number of Broadband Users Multiplied by the Average Number in all Other Countries	96.83	184.56	0.00	954.30

Table 3. Econometric Models of Openness

Explanatory Variables	Model 1	Model 2	Model 3	Model 4
Number of Broadband Users per 100 People	0.5410 (0.0680)	0.3920 (0.0880)		
Number of Broadband Users times Average Number in all Other Countries			0.0231 (0.0030)	0.0194 (0.0039)
Wald Test for the Country Fixed Effects	$F=275.11$ $p = 0.000$	$F=306.58$ $p = 0.000$	$F=263.29$ $p = 0.000$	$F=293.89$ $p = 0.000$
Wald Test for the Year Fixed Effects	Not Included	$F=14.29$ $p = 0.000$	Not Included	$F=14.94$ $p = 0.000$
Number of Observations	1,776	1,776	1,776	1,776
R^2	0.9375	0.9417	0.9377	0.9421
AIC	14519.86	14418.73	14514.86	14407.63

Note: The dependent variable for all of the models is the ratio of a country's trade (imports plus exports) to its GDP in a particular year. Robust standard errors reported in parentheses.

Table 4. Sensitivity Analysis for Econometric Estimates

Variation of the Model	Estimated Coefficient on Broadband Term	AIC	Comments
Model 4 in Table 3	0.0194 (0.0039)	14407.63	
Added Country's Share of World GDP	0.0196 (0.0041)	14409.54	Coefficient on additional variable not significantly different from zero.
Added an Indicator for WTO Membership	0.0196 (0.0039)	14408.91	Coefficient on additional variable not significantly different from zero.
Less Restricted Coefficient:		14409.46	Wald Test does not reject that the two groups have the same value of γ: the F statistic is 0.17, and the p value is 0.6779.
High Income Countries	0.0195 (0.0039)		
Developing Countries	0.0159 (0.0092)		
Contemporaneous, Rather than Lagged, Value of the Broadband Measure	0.0176 (0.0038)	14412.11	

Table 5. Historical Effects on the Countries' Openness to Trade

	Increase in the trade-to-GDP ratio due to the increase in broadband users (2001-2012)	Total increase in openness to trade (2001-2012)
Simple average over all 148 countries	4.21	9.51
Average over the 44 high income countries	10.21	9.32
Average over the 104 developing countries	1.67	9.58
The ten countries with the largest historical contributions		
Switzerland	17.34	9.48
Netherlands	17.30	38.89
Denmark	16.79	16.61
Korea	16.03	45.98
Norway	15.78	-6.12
France	15.65	1.50
Iceland	15.33	34.03
Luxembourg	14.77	49.81
United Kingdom	14.45	9.60
Belgium	14.33	19.11

Table 6. Comparison of Econometric Models 4 and 2

	Increase in the trade-to-GDP ratio due to the historical increase in broadband users, based on preferred model 4 with network effects	Increase in the trade-to-GDP ratio due to the historical increase in broadband users, based on alternative model 2 without network effects
Simple average over all 148 countries	4.21	3.59
Average over the 44 high income countries	10.21	8.64
Average over the 104 developing countries	1.67	1.46

Table 7. Econometric Models of Year-to-Year Increases in the Number of Broadband Users

Explanatory Variables	Model 5	Model 6	Model 7	Model 8
Constant	0.7691 (0.0355)	0.4958 (0.0295)	0.2944 (0.0274)	0.2936 (0.0265)
Lagged Number of Broadband Users		0.0637 (0.0053)		0.0021 (0.0090)
Real GDP per Capita			0.0041 (0.0003)	0.0041 (0.0005)
Number of Observations	1,867	1,867	1,867	1,867
R^2	0.0000	0.1164	0.2190	0.2190
AIC	6899.606	6670.515	6440.215	6442.072

Note: The dependent variable for all of the models is the year-to-year change in each country's number of broadband users per 100 people. Robust standard errors reported in parentheses.

Table 8. Projected Future Effect on Openness to Trade

	Projected increase in the number of broadband users over the next five years	Increase in the trade-to-GDP ratio due to the increase in broadband users over the next five years
Simple average over all 148 countries	4.47	3.20
Average over the 44 high income countries	9.59	6.88
Average over the 104 developing countries	2.34	1.67
The ten countries with the largest combined effects		
Luxembourg	23.79	13.40
Norway	20.39	12.97
Switzerland	17.84	12.24
Denmark	13.37	10.24
Qatar	19.35	9.72
Netherlands	11.11	9.16
Sweden	13.22	9.07
France	10.20	8.80
Belgium	10.64	8.51
Australia	13.29	8.44